S

A NOTE ABOUT THE TEXT

Muhammad Ali was born with the name Cassius Marcellus Clay, Jr., on January 17, 1942, in Louisville, Kentucky. After winning a 1960 Olympic gold medal, he arrived on the boxing scene as a kind of prophet—larger than life, larger than just a sports hero—whose coming foretold a new era of African American empowerment. Though Ali is a Muslim, like all great prophets he transcends his own faith with the power of his message. He speaks to all people of all faiths.

Ali's boxing career spanned more than twenty years and included the impressive feat of becoming the first three-time Heavyweight Champion of the World. Because this is a picture book for very young readers, it is not comprehensive but focuses on his most inspiring fights—his first match with Sonny Liston in 1964 and the Rumble in the Jungle with George Foreman in 1974.

At the time of this book's publication, Ali is living in Scottsdale, Arizona. Though his speech and movements have been slowed by Parkinson's disease (a result of being hit in the ring), there is still a twinkle in his eye, revealing the inner brilliance that fueled the most amazing boxing career—and one of the most original lives—in history.

FOR MUHAMMAD ALI —J.W.

Text copyright © 2007 by Jonah Winter • Illustrations copyright © 2007 by François Roca • All rights reserved. Published in the United States by SCHWARTZ & WADE BOOKS, an imprint of Random House Children's Books, a division of Random House, Inc., New York • SCHWARTZ & WADE and colophon are trademarks of Random House, Inc. • www.randomhouse.com/kids • Educators and librarians, for a variety of teaching tools, visit us at www.randomhouse.com/teachers • Library of Congress Cataloging-in-Publication Data • Winter, Jonah. Muhammad Ali : champion of the world / Jonah Winter ; illustrated by François Roca. — 1st ed. • p. cm. ISBN 978-0-375-83622-0 (trade) — ISBN 978-0-375-93787-3 (lib. bdg.) • 1. Ali, Muhammad, 1942– —Juvenile literature. 2. Boxers (Sports)—United States—Biography—Juvenile literature. • I. Roca, François, ill. II. Title. GV1132.A44W56 2008 • 796.83092—dc22 • [B] 2006101855 • The text of this book is set in Ideologica and Cablegram. • The illustrations are rendered in oil paint. • Book design by Rachael Cole

PRINTED IN CHINA

1 3 7 9 10 8 6 4 2

First Edition

MUHAMMAD ALI
CHAMPION OF THE WORLD

WRITTEN BY **JONAH WINTER**
ILLUSTRATED BY **FRANÇOIS ROCA**

schwartz & wade books • new york

IN THE BEGINNING was Jack Johnson,
and Jack Johnson was **THE MAN—**
the first black king in the Kingdom of Boxing.
But after defeating the Great White Hope . . .

Jack Johnson was hated and booed
all over America
just for the color of his skin
and for acting proud—
and so he wandered off to a distant land.

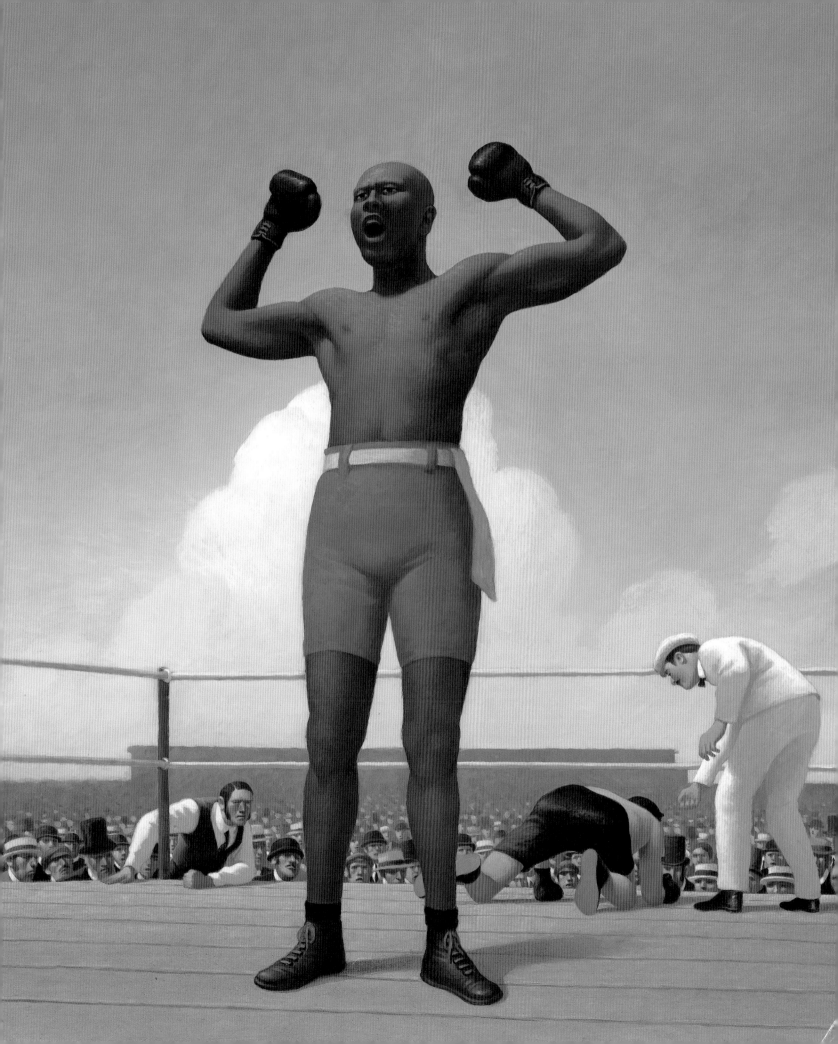

And some many years later,
in a different age, God said,

**LET THERE BE
JOE LOUIS,**

for the world was now ready
for another black champion.

JOE LOUIS

The B

And Joe Louis appeared and was called

THE BROWN BOMBER,

but he was more like a **TANK.**

With fists of steel, he slugged his way
to the throne of power.

And some many years later,
there came another mighty king,
named Sonny Liston,

SONNY LISTON

who existed for only one purpose:
to knock people out in the very first round.

And God said, **IS THAT ALL THERE IS . . .**
TO A BOXER?

And the heavens opened up,
and there appeared a great man
descending on a cloud, jump-roping
into the Kingdom of Boxing.
And he was called **CASSIUS CLAY.**

And Cassius Clay said,
"I WILL BE THE GREATEST OF ALL TIME."

Then he **TALKED**
and **JIVED**
and **PRACTICED**
and **PUNCHED** his way to victory,

until he had won the Olympic gold medal.

And Clay said,

**"I'M GOING TO TALK AND TALK AND TALK,
AND THE WORLD'S GOING TO KNOW MY NAME."**

For he believed in himself
and believed he would be triumphant.

And the World said,

**WHO IS THIS MAN
WHO BRAGS ABOUT HIMSELF?
SURELY HE IS FULL OF HOT AIR!
SURELY HE SHOULD KEEP HIS BIG MOUTH SHUT!**

But Cassius Clay did **NOT** keep his big mouth shut.
He said he could beat
the great Sonny Liston,
Heavyweight Champion of the World.

He said, **"SONNY LISTON'S JUST A BIG UGLY BEAR,"**
and he brought him a big bear collar.

He said, **"THEY SAY SONNY LISTON IS GREAT,
BUT HE MUST FALL TO ME IN EIGHT"**
(eight rounds, that is).

And the World said,
**YOU'RE OUT OF YOUR MIND!
LISTON WILL KNOCK YOU
OUT OF THE RING!**

And Cassius Clay said,
**"FLOAT LIKE A BUTTERFLY, STING LIKE A BEE,
YOU CAN'T HIT WHAT YOU CAN'T SEE."**

And sure enough, on the night of the Big Fight,

Liston was swinging at air

as Cassius Clay danced this way and that,

TALKING and **TALKING, TEASING,**

luring Liston to wear himself out, then—

POW!–

letting loose with a flurry of punches

that shocked the World

into silence.

When the bell rang at the end of round six,
Liston just sat in his corner,
and he would not get up.

And Cassius Clay said,

"I AM KING OF THE WORLD! I AM THE GREATEST!!!"

And there before the masses

stood a great shining man,

clad in white silk.

With a voice as beautiful as rivers,

Cassius Clay announced that he was changing his name.

Clay had been the name of the white slave master

who had owned his African ancestors.

From this moment on,

he would no longer use a white man's name.

With flashbulbs flashing,

Cassius Clay announced his brand-new name:

MUHAMMAD ALI.

This name came from his new religion: Islam.
Islam was from Africa,
the homeland of his ancestors,
before they were brought to America
in slave boats.

And all across the land,
there were others
just as proud of their African roots
and their Islamic faith.
They were called the Nation of Islam,
and they were part of a great wave of people
who would not be silenced anymore.
And Muhammad Ali became their prophet.

And while other boxers were **PUMMELING** each other
left and right,

**GROWLING, SPITTING, SLUGGING, GRUNTING,
SPLATTERING BLOOD** in the Kingdom of Boxing . . .

Muhammad Ali was **DANCING** in the ring,

TALKING and **TALKING** and **TALKING** and **TALKING.**
He recited poems about how great he was.
He spoke out against racism.
And this made some people mad and *very* mad.
Boxers were supposed to be big dumb brutes.
African Americans were supposed to know their place
and keep their mouths shut.
But Muhammad Ali was a new kind of boxer—
and a new kind of person.
And he was creating a new way
for African Americans to be:
PROUD, STRONG,
and **WILLING TO FIGHT.**

Then one day it came to pass

that the American army

told him he must fight in a war.

Muhammad Ali said, **NO.**

Boxing was one thing,

but killing people was wrong.

And so . . . the greatest boxer who ever lived

was hauled into a courtroom,

where he was banished

from the Kingdom of Boxing,

and stripped of his title,

Heavyweight Champion of the World.

And the judge said,

**YOU ARE NOT ALLOWED TO BOX
FOR FIVE WHOLE YEARS.
IT'S JAIL TIME FOR YOU.**

And the World said,

**YOU'RE ALL THROUGH,
YOU'RE FINISHED,
YOU'LL NEVER MAKE A COMEBACK.**

And for three years,
Ali went to different courtrooms,
fighting for his right to box,
fighting for his freedom—and finally
winning this battle,
LIKE THE CHAMPION HE WAS.

And in a flash,
the prophet reappeared,
jump-roping back into the Kingdom of Boxing,
And he said,
"I AM THE GREATEST."

And he **BOXED,**
and he **DANCED,**
and he **TALKED**
his way back, all the way . . .

to the greatest fight **EVER**
in the Kingdom of Boxing:
the Rumble in the Jungle,
live from the homeland of his ancestors—
Africa.

To be crowned King in Africa
was Ali's dream.
He would be the bridge that joined
Africans and African Americans.
But first he had to beat . . .

the mighty GEORGE FOREMAN,
who was younger,
stronger,
and meaner than Ali.
And the World said,
MUHAMMAD ALI DOES NOT STAND A CHANCE!

And Ali answered with a brand-new poem:

"I HAVE WRESTLED WITH AN ALLIGATOR,
I DONE TUSSLED WITH A WHALE.
I DONE HANDCUFFED LIGHTNING
AND THROWED THUNDER IN JAIL."

But when the bell rang,
and the fight began,
the great Ali lay crumpled on the ropes
as George Foreman pummeled him.
No one knew
that this was just a trick
by the sly Ali
called ROPE-A-DOPE— by round eight,
the mighty George Foreman had punched
and punched and punched away all his strength.

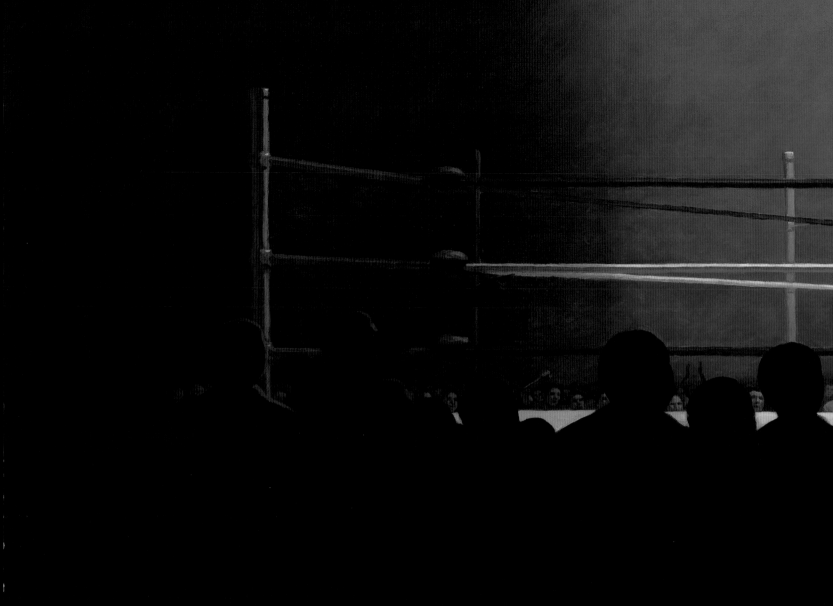

Then God said, **IT IS TIME.**

And in a flash of lightning,
Ali **WOKE UP** from his trick
and **SPRANG** from the ropes.

With thousands of Africans chanting his name,
Ali **KNOCKED** George Foreman to the mat.
And just like that,

Muhammad Ali was once again

CHAMPION OF THE WORLD.

And though he could barely stand,
he lifted his arms above his head and said,

"I AM THE GREATEST."

And his people held him high
in their arms, and rejoiced—
for his victory was more
than just a boxing victory.
It was a triumph of imagination.
He believed he was

THE GREATEST,

and he believed in the greatness of his people.
And there in the center of Africa,
they crowned their King.